OUR DEVILISH ALCOHOLIC PERSONALITIES

by

The Author of *The Little Red Book*

Our
Devilish Alcoholic
Personalities

by

The Author of *The Little Red Book*

HAZELDEN
Box 176 • Center City, Minnesota 55012

First Hazelden Printing, 1975
Second Printing, 1976
Third Printing, 1977

ISBN: 0-89486-008-9
International Copyright © 1970
By Hamar Publishers

Printed and Manufactured in the
United States of America

DEDICATION

This book is dedicated to A.A. members worldwide. To the newcomers who are the life blood of our fellowship and to the oldtimers who are its backbone.

Ed. W.

ACKNOWLEDGMENTS

It would not have been possible to present the issues in this book without the generous help and cooperation of many friends, to whom I humbly express my great appreciation.

Acknowledgment is likewise extended to the following publishing houses and individuals who have granted me permission to paraphrase pertinent material from their publications, and in three instances to reprint short articles.

Austin Ripley, Colfax, Wisconsin; Amelia Lane, Chicago, Illinois; Harper & Row publishers, New York, N.Y.; A.A. Grapevine, New York, N.Y.; The Reader's Digest, Pleasantville, New York, N.Y.; Appleton-Century-Crofts, Inc., New York, N.Y.

This is not an official A.A. book, but it does deal with practical application of The Twelve Steps which have brought sobriety and peace of mind to many members, including the author. For this, I am deeply indebted to the founders of Alcoholics Anonymous.

NOTES

NOTES

NOTES

NOTES

CONTENTS

The Dedication 5

Acknowledgments 7

The Author's Story 11

ODAP, The Alcoholic Monkey 28

The Alcoholic Paradox 59

The Quietest Room in Town 61

Landmarks in A.A. History 64

Alcohol. Facts and Misconceptions about
    its effect upon the Alcoholic 67

New Slants on Old A.A. Ideas 70

One Alcoholic's Version of
    The Lord's Prayer 78

The Author's Story

For many years, I lived the miserable, unpredictable life of a drinking alcoholic. My name is unimportant. Today, the only thing of importance, to me, is that I am an arrested alcoholic.

Thanks to God, as I understand Him, and to the help of our A.A. Program, I have not used alcohol, as a beverage, since December 13, 1941. This statement is not made in a boastful manner. It is engendered by gratitude for the daily sobriety which I enjoy.

I was born in a small river town in Northern Wisconsin. The doctor who delivered me said that I was born cold sober. He claimed that I arrived in this world without the slightest trace of gin, beer, wine or whiskey upon my breath. This was a condition which John Barleycorn changed for me later.

Apparently, there was no plausible reason for my addiction to alcohol. None of the members of my family drank. To the contrary, they were sober, religious-minded persons of good moral standards and highly respected in our community. As a child, I lacked nothing, either of material things, or social contacts.

Our home atmosphere abounded with love and mutual interests in each other with a firm background of religious training for all. Alcoholic beverages were never kept in our home, nor were they ever indulged in by any members of my family. —

My parents lived serious, dedicated Christian lives, and they tried to influence my life accordingly. Their plan worked for a few years, but as I grew older, I rebelled against this strict spiritual regimentation. When this happened, they used well-meant but misguided force to steer me along the path of spiritual instruction.

The razorstrap was in vogue in those days, and I received liberal applications of the strap whenever I became too contankerous and contaminated with sin. Since my association with organized religion was compulsory, I quickly dropped it when I left home, at the early age of seventeen.

I had always been taught that drinking was a cardinal sin, and that bars, saloons and nightclubs were believed to be sordid dens of iniquity, also that the persons who frequented them were immoral, undesirable citizens.

This could have been partly true, but half-truths for an adventurous young fellow like myself, were dangerous, challenging paths to tread. Invariably I chose the wrong half, namely; the bad half.

This was particularly true after I was discharged from naval service. A New York friend got me a sales position which permitted me to travel and afforded me a large expense account for entertainment of my customers.

I traveled over much of the United States and parts of Canada where the opportunity to investigate these dens of iniquity became a part of my life, and investigate them I did for many years—both day and night.

My findings were astounding. Instead of sordid, vulgar places, many of them were elegant beyond description. Words are inadequate to describe their attractive, polished mahogany bars over-hung with huge crystal chandeliers —to say nothing of the immaculate back bars covered with clean shining glasses.

Surely, my parents had misguided me about these places, as well as the people I met in them. With the exception of a few rum-soaked souls, they were not immoral, shady characters. To the contrary, many of them were vivacious, interesting and often cultured individuals. These people did not drink in a sinful, gluttonous manner, but rather in a happy, convivial bond of good-fellowship.

I loved this atmosphere and enjoyed it for many years. Alcohol brought me that warm, mellow, glow, so dear to an alcoholic. Sort of a Fool's Paradise — an Alcoholic Utopia that later was lost, but one which I spent many years trying to regain, without success, but I kept on trying.

My sales record was excellent when I was sober. This appeased my ego, but it prevented me from facing the reality that I was seldom sober. With true alcoholic rationalization, I decided that by moving to a new territory my heavy drinking would cease, and that I could drink normally again. I felt that my customers were at fault, so I asked to be transferred to a different territory.

My company accepted a request for transfer

and I was given a Northwest territory with headquarters in Minneapolis. The idea that I could run away from alcohol was a great mistake, for it seemed there were as many bars and drinking customers in the new territory as in the one I had just left.

Several years later, I learned from the "Big Book," Alcoholics Anonymous that I was laboring under the false impression that I could become a controlled drinker. It stated that many alcoholics continue in their flights from reality until either alcoholic death, or lunacy are imminent. In some cases the unfortunate addict falls prey to both of these extremities.

This was exactly the direction I was headed, but being ignorant of the fact, I would have savagely ridiculed the audacity of anyone who even intimated such a thing. Chronic alcoholics invariably react that way. Medical authorities labelled alcoholism a physical and mental disease, but I avoided all thoughts of having such a disease.

Nevertheless, I was experiencing considerable physical difficulty in driving at times. Business trips that should have required only days to complete often took me a week, because of hangovers that made me too jittery to travel.

Apparently, the hourglass of my control over liquor had about run out. It took no supermind to account for my erratic behavior, yet I refused to observe the danger signal.

This seemed to worry everybody but me. My district sales manager was most concerned. He did not approve of the inroads drinking was making upon my services and told me so. In self defence, I promised to quit drinking during business hours.

Realizing that total abstinence was the only way to retain my position I, somehow, managed to keep sober for ten days, and during this period I secured the largest contract for company products ever taken in my territory.

What a wonderful break, I thought. Dame Fortune has smiled upon me at last. I'd better hurry back to the office with my contract and show how indispensable I am to my organization.

The office was eight miles away. I started back with the best of intentions, but stopped at a bar for one drink. Ten days later, I returned home unable to tell where I'd been, or what I'd been doing.

Suffice it to say, the district sales manager knew, and he immediately notified the division office in Chicago that my services with the company should be terminated. They agreed, promising to send an official to Minneapolis within thirty days to discharge me. It was a hectic day to say the least.

Seemingly sick unto death, I managed to return home where I lay on a couch in my front sunroom masked in a ten-day growth of beard. In complete exhaustion, I lay there helpless to defend myself. There was no reasonable excuse for my condition. Shame, remorse, humiliation and fear all contributed to a devastating feeling of frustration.

My addiction to alcohol had cut off much rapport with relatives, friends and business associates. Prior to this, brawls, drunkenness, auto accidents and absenteeism from work warned of danger ahead, but they only served to increase my drinking.

17

In football we excuse the player who makes a fumble. It is hard, however, to forgive the player who defeats his team by running the ball back to his own goal for a touchdown. My daily drinking was comparable to such stupidity, as each morning I awakened with the physical sensation of having gone through a cement mixer loaded with coarse gravel, only to continue drinking where I had left off the night before.

My situation was deplorable. It seemed that Dame Fortune had completely deserted me. In a way, she had, but it was just a temporary affair, as she had been working through my wife who had been praying for a solution of my drinking problem.

At that time A. A. was quite new in Minneapolis, and had been receiving broad publicity in our local newspaper regarding the manner in which alcoholics could be helped.

I avoided reading these articles, but not my wife. She garnered much hope and information from them. So, as I lay dying after my ten day drinking orgy, she popped the question: "Do you wish to keep on drinking, or would you like to call A. A. for help?"

What a tragic end to my alcoholic ego! I wanted help, all right, but my pride (false pride) interfered with asking for it. Finally, in utter desperation, I told her to call A. A. for me. "No," she said, "That isn't the way it's done. You call." Since I'd lost my glasses, calling was impossible, so she finally took pity on me and made the call.

In 1941 the Minneapolis fellowship was young, inexperienced and hard pressed to handle the hundreds of calls for help that were coming in. Consequently, sponsorship action was often delayed, and, of necessity, a haphazard endeavor at the best.

My case was the exception. It brought immediate and most startling results. Within the hour, two nondescript gentlemen appeared at our door. Their appearance was so unusual that my wife questioned the advisability of allowing them in.

Today, hippies with long hair and dirty clothes are no uncommon sight, but twenty-eight years ago they were seldom, if ever, accepted in polite society.

These gentlemen were both bewhiskered and

19

shabbily dressed. My sponsor (to be) sported a long handlebar mustache with sharp points turned up at each end. He stood five feet eight inches tall and weighed about two hundred and forty pounds, as he walked around my death bed. He didn't breathe like most human beings —he just panted and groaned. In my jittery, weakened condition, he looked so much like the devil I wondered if I hadn't by-passed death and had arrived in hell physically intact.

My opinion of A.A. had been poor to start with, but it fell to a new low after seeing this representative of the fellowship. Right then, I decided that it was much worse than I had suspected — that it must be some sort of a dirty, hairy cult. Full of self-pity and with a completely negative outlook on life, I bemoaned my terrible fate.

As much as I abhorred the appearance of my sponsor (to be) he had certain favorable traits to his credit. He showed a genuine interest in my predicament and he spoke my language without preaching to me.

He insisted that I be hospitalized, which I objected to, as I had no money and told him I couldn't see how the bill would ever be paid.

He said, "In your condition, you are in no position to think. I'll help you. Come along with me and let me think for you."

His assurance brought little hope to me. I was so exhausted, both physically and mentally, I could neither disagree nor fight back, so I dressed and went along with him, wondering what would happen next.

A guilty conscience complicated my morbid fears. My spirit seemed broken beyond repair, but with such mentality as I had left, I decided it would be more profitable to join A.A. and raise whiskers than to prolong my hellish suffering alone at home.

The A.A. Club House, at that time, was on the first floor of a tiny four-room apartment on Park Avenue. It was a run-down, uninviting place which A.A. got because nobody else wanted it. It was the flat in which some of the Dillinger gang made their last stand with Minneapolis police. Bullet holes from this encounter were still in the walls. I could have cared less, as I lay there on a cot until evening.

Today, viewing the matter in retrospect, it surely was an appropriate setting in which to make my last stand against John Barleycorn. I fared much better than the Dillinger gang, because they lost, and it was the beginning of a new life for me.

In 1941 Minneapolis hospitals were not too receptive to alcoholic patients. As a result, prospective sponsors often carried with them goof balls, pills and liquor to alleviate the misery of alcohol withdrawal from A.A. newcomers.

The lack of hospital admittance did not deter my sponsor's efforts to make me comfortable. He was equal to the occasion which he met by administering two ounces of whiskey to me every hour until evening, when a hospital room was available. In other words, he kept me plastered all day in order to officially sober me up later.

It was a painful, frustrating experience which I shall never forget; an ordeal which few members went through at that time. A.A. newcomers should thank God for the medical facilities today and the fact that alcoholism is treated as an illness rather than a sin.

Since there is nothing permanent in life, I was released from the hospital within a few days, under two provisos. *Number One —* that I immediately start attending A.A. meetings. *Num-*

ber Two — that I make monthly payments to the hospital until my bill was paid. I agreed and faithfully complied with both provisions.

My contact with the members of A.A. was most stimulating and exciting, and despite the fact that the blind were leading the blind, we made daily progress. Some failures occurred, but their numbers were small compared to the members who succeeded.

I was most fortunate to become part of a squad of desperate "last gaspers," to whom the book, "Alcoholics Anonymous," had become their only authority for the recovery from alcoholism. Each member knew that to drink again meant slow alcoholic death, but that drinking could be averted by study of the book "Alcoholics Anonymous" to learn the working mechanics of the Twelve Steps.

Fundamental instructions relative to the application of the Twelve Steps became necessary as our membership increased. Some members didn't own Big Books; other members qualified as alcoholics (according to Step Number One) but skipped the rest of the steps, except that part of Step Twelve which says to carry the message to alcoholics. Their ignorance of

23

the A.A. program gave them but little message to carry.

The Founders of the original Minneapolis A.A. group, realizing the need of instructions for its new members, set up a series of classes for that purpose. Older members conducted these classes in four consecutive weeks of what they called, indoctrination classes.

After two years, it was decided by the officers of the group that I was qualified to conduct one of these classes. Their decision appealed to my alcoholic ego, of course, but it demanded a close study of the manner in which the Book, "Alcoholics Anonymous," suggested the steps should be lived. Since one cannot impart to another something he does not understand himself, I compiled notes from which I gave lectures on all of the Twelve Steps.

Visiting members from A.A. groups in the United States and Canada often sat in on these meetings. Invariably, they requested copies of my notes for use in their groups.

Since these notes were useless to other members without clarification they were enlarged into book form entitled, "An Interpretation Of The Twelve Steps Of The A.A. Program." In

1949 this name was changed to "The Little Red Book." *

My friends were delighted with the accomplishment, but I could not share their feelings for the question of authority to have written such an interpretation of the Twelve Steps bothered me.

During the years 1944, 1945, 1946 and 1947 the members of our A.A. group established a yearly recreational event which they named, "The A.A. Founders Outing."

Invitations to participate in a two-week outing at a large summer resort in Northern Minnesota were accepted by many founders of A.A. groups in the United States and Canada. Doctor Bob, co-founder of A.A. and his wife Anne were among those who honored us with their presence.

Viewing the outing in retrospect, it must be regarded as a part of the good old days in A.A. for those of us who attended it. Both Doctor Bob and Anne have since passed away, but the memory of their warm friendship will always remain with us.

* The Little Red Book available from Hazelden, Box 11 Center City, Minnesota 55012.

We still have pleasant recollections of Doctor Bob pitching horse shoes with our members and of Anne sitting in the lounge visiting with our wives and discussing the need of cooperation with their husbands in A.A.

In 1946 my friend Barry C. drove to Akron, Ohio leaving the manuscript of "The Little Red Book" with Doctor Bob who wrote me shortly afterwards that he thought the book would be most helpful to our members. Barry established credit with a local publisher and the book was printed in August 1946.* Doctor Bob's opinion of "Stools & Bottles" is not known as he passed away before the book was published.

Having supplied two books to help our new members acquire an understanding of the practical application of the Twelve Steps, it seemed that my sponsorship efforts, in that direction, had been fulfilled. It was a pleasant feeling, and my alcoholic mind welcomed the opportunity to rest upon my laurels.

Recently, however, in checking my files, I discovered a large accumulation of A.A. notes;

* Stools & Bottles available from Hazelden, Box 11, Center City, Minnesota 55012

also recorded talks, that I have given to A.A. groups in years gone by. Two questions arose: Wasn't I becoming complacent? Shouldn't I share this history with my A.A. friends.

Meditating upon these questions, my conscience replied, "YES." It said, "Get busy and share your best efforts with other alcoholics as you are supposed to do."

It is with deep gratitude for the sobriety that A.A. has given me for so many years that I present this new book, "Our Devilish Alcoholic Personalities." May it bring fond reminiscence to the oldtimers in our fellowship, and helpful inspiration to our newcomers.

ODAP
THE ALCOHOLIC MONKEY

The year was 1935. An historical event of in--
ternational consequence was in the making.
The principal characters were two sick men
whose addiction to alcohol superseded all
other interests in life.

Now these men were total strangers who lived
several hundred miles from each other. One's
name was Bill and the other's was Doctor Bob.

In May of 1935, as though moved by some
miraculous power, they met in the city of
Akron, Ohio, where they founded a fellowship
known to this day as Alcoholics Anonymous.

Their purpose was to keep sober and by the
example of their sobriety to help kindred suf-
ferers recover from alcoholism. They accom-
plished this by living a simple Twelve Step program which treated the physical, mental and
spiritual symptoms of their illness.

Although medical treatment was required, the
crux of their incredible success depended upon
the spiritual condition of each member. *Will*

Power was not a factor of recovery, as their only will was to drink.

Faced by this grave extremity, they decided that their help must come from some power greater than alcohol. So they chose the only alternative of desperate, dying men — help from "God as they understood HIM."

It was an honest, sincere choice, but it presented many obstacles as it called for surrender of certain character defects, Such surrender was hard to achieve by men subservient to the daily dictates of a lower alcoholic power for so many years.

So it came to pass that a hostile little MENTAL MONKEY named ODAP subtly invaded the ranks of A.A. where he still clings to the shoulders of its members whispering harmful anti-sober temptations into their ears.

Now "ODAP'S" appearance in A.A. was not exactly coincidental. Actually he was an offspring of OUR DEVILISH ALCOHOLIC PERSONALITIES. None of us was born with these personalities. We developed them throughout many years of uncontrolled drinking.

ODAP'S name was coined from the first letter

29

of each of these four words. Namely: "O" from *Our*, "D" from *Devilish*, "A" from *Alcoholic*, and "P" from *Personalities*. Added in proper sequence these letters spell "ODAP."

So, it goes without saying that "ODAP" was well qualified to keep our members fearful and unhappy, in spite of their best efforts to avoid him. His daily inroads upon their sobriety caused some members to drink again.

It was a most confusing situation. A.A. advocated that sobriety came from GOD, as the members understood Him; whereas, it seemed that drunkenness must come from some other power. Among the serious thinking members a big question arose. Was it possible that there were *two powers* in A.A.? *A Higher Power* and *A Lower Power?*

Obviously, the answer was — Yes. But the members then and now often fail to recognize this fact.

Too often each member fights a battle against himself, with that diabolic monkey ODAP clinging to his shoulder whispering urges to drink into his ears.

When an alcoholic seeks help from A.A. to recover from his illness, ODAP cries out in a loud voice against it.

"Don't get mixed up with that bunch of low-browed, degenerate weaklings. Use your own will power. You can stop drinking if you want to. Try a little controlled drinking."

"Try anything, but stay out of A.A. If you join that group of reformers you'll have to stop drinking entirely and you certainly won't like that."

His bad counseling keeps too many helpless alcoholics out of A.A. Some die needlessly as he inflates their egos with absurd opinions of their importance and superiority over other drunks.

Those who do get into A.A. and acquire daily sobriety for awhile, feel safe, but it is a false security with ODAP constantly inciting them to fall off the wagon.

At this point I will no longer generalize upon the matter but will give you my personal experience with this detestable little ape, in A.A.

Step One infuriated him. He jumped up and down upon my back pounding me upon my head yelling his objections into my ears.

31

"You are not sick! You are not powerless! Your life is not unmanageable! Suppose you did drink too much. All you need is some food and a good night of rest, then you'll be Okay."

Finally in utter desperation, I admitted that alcohol had me licked and that my life was out of control. It took this despicable situation to give me the needed humility to accept Step One and to seriously consider working Step Two.

Step Number Two enraged ODAP. He used all of his underhanded, cunning technique to discourage my acceptance of this Step.

He raged and raved, and strangely enough, some of his objections made good sense to my jittery, bewildered mind.

"You're not insane," he told me. "There's nothing wrong with your mind and don't let those A.A. nitwits tell you otherwise. It's a silly, insulting program, to say the least."

"They are as crazy as that policeman you ran into at a highway intersection while you were driving without a license on the wrong side of a two-way street. You are not insane. That could happened to anybody."

ODAP was in constant disagreement with all my best efforts to live the Twelve Steps, Step Three especially. This Step "bugged" him severely and he emphatically told me so.

"You've done lots of idiotic things, but nothing like turning your life over to the care of God," he advised me.

"What are these people? They must be a bunch of holy-rollers. Have no part of their fellowship."

"You don't need God. What you need is a good psychiatrist. He'll give you the cause of alcoholism, *providing, of course, you are really an alcoholic.*"

"First Things First — easy does it. Don't rush into this spiritual business too fast."

He had me as mixed up as the English alcoholic female that a rescue squad found one night during the war. She was nude and drunk in the basement of a bombed London building. She just stood there muttering to herself.

"I don't understand. I don't understand." "What is it that you don't understand?" they asked.

"Well I was a bit intoxicated, so I took my bottle with me and got into the bath tub. I finished my bath, took a last drink, reached over and pulled out the bath plug and the whole bloody house fell down on me. I don't understand — I just don't understand!"

I didn't understand either with ODAP around telling me that A.A. was nothing more than a religious organization, and at first, I believed him.

So I listened to his advice. This put me on the wrong track and prevented my immediate acceptance of Step Three.

"Read less and less in that A.A. Book, and more and more books on medicine and psychology. They have all your answers," ODAP told me.

This sounded reasonable, but I noticed later that members who followed his advice came to know more and more about less and less until they knew nothing about anything, except *getting drunk*.

From their sad experiences, I decided that the founders of A.A. knew what they were doing when they put Step Three into our program. So I accepted it wholeheartedly.

Personally, I never did look upon A.A. as a religion. In my opinion, it represented a spiritual way of life by which alcoholics could recover from their physical and mental illness.

My early religious training, as I understood it, was intended to save souls. A.A. had no such objective, it's main purpose was to save lives, and to unite families.

ODAP gave strong disapproval when I decided to carry out the provisions of Step Four. At this point he had me half agreeing with him that a written inventory was unnecessary, giving the following reasons to substantiate his disapproval.

"Better think hard before you act on this step, old buddy, you can't record all of your bad actions. That's a negative approach — psychologically, it's the wrong thing to do."

"A.A. is apparently misnamed. It's not a recovery program. It is a defeatists program. You don't have to make a written inventory. A mental inventory is just as good."

"You have no flaws in your make-up. You are not a weakling like the other drunks in A.A. Be positive. Don't admit defeat."

35

"But if you are too weak-willed to fight the issue, go ahead, write an inventory. Leave out the bad points. Just list the good ones. You've got lots of them."

I was so accustomed to this sort of alcoholic rationalization that I delayed taking Step Four as long as possible.

Finally, I did make my inventory. It undoubtedly wasn't the best in the world, but it served to overcome my obstinacy and to lessen my battle against surrender.

Step Five brought out ODAP's real demoniacal impulses. He struck out at me with his best verbal punches to stop any attempt I might make to take Step Five.

"You can't trust your drinking history with another human being," he told me. "Your record is too bad. You'll be lucky if they don't put you in jail."

"Why risk it? Why humiliate yourself? Why not forget this whole silly matter about confiding with another human being?"

"You are the only one who knows anything about your past behavior. Let the memories die a natural death. Why tell some disinterested clergyman about them?"

"Skip the matter. Who is going to be the wiser if you don't disclose the wrongs you have committed? You have admitted them to yourself. That's enough."

If ODAP had any redemptive characteristics they are unknown to our members. We must admit, however, that his tenacity to louse up our attempts to keep sober, and happy, is beyond all power of human conception.

His hypnotic power to dull our spiritual enthusiasm over Steps Six and Seven becomes a threat to our hopes for daily progress in A. A.

He does this in a clever, most convincing manner after we have taken the first Five Steps, by advising us to ease up on our efforts.

His plan often works out, but to our loss, as he encourages us to believe that because we no longer drink, that we are now cured of alcoholism.

He talks to us about the things we love to hear, and tells us that there is no need for further concern and instructs us the battle is won.

37

"You've gotten rid of the alcoholic termites," he says, "Don't become too concerned over a few helpless cockroaches."

"Slow up a bit. Remember the A.A. motto, "Easy does it." All you joined A.A. for was sobriety. You've got it now, so stop taking yourself so seriously."

"You're not supposed to become a saint. Don't try to grow wings. Act natural, so grumble and raise a little hell once in awhile. Everyone else is doing it."

"You've been in A.A. quite awhile. You're entitled to an occasional slip. Go ahead — have fun."

"God knows you're human. He'll forgive you and the A.A. members will take care of you if you get drunk."

"You've got it made now. There's nothing to worry about any more. You owe your drinking customers more entertainment then they have received lately. Don't ostracize yourself from them, or you won't have any customers left."

"In fact, you can do a little social drinking when your business demands it. Drinking is no longer a problem for you. You've proved that you can take it or leave it alone."

ODAP knows this isn't true. He knows it is a lie, yet he tricks many gullible, recovering alcoholics into believing it, and in this manner transforms their sober thinking into drinking thinking.

Procrastination is a cunning trick he uses to promote drinking. Step Eight gives ODAP an excellent opportunity to get in his hatchet work on newcomers. Few of them are anxious to list the people they have harmed, and even less anxious to consider making amends to them. ODAP encourages their reluctance to comply with such action.

"You are not ready to take this step. What's your hurry?" he asked me. "Suppose you make such a list and your wife accidentally finds it. What happens then?"

"Your wife is pretty nosey, you know. She's bound to find that list, sooner or later. Remember her suspicious nature? You'll be subject to her nagging the rest of your life."

"Don't take the chance. Don't make a list. Whatever harm you have done is over. Carry

39

in your mind the old adage; never put into writing anything you don't want the whole world to know about."

"A written list could boomerang upon you, and become a future source of trouble and embarrassment. Be smart, and don't jeopardize your reputation. This step may be okay for other alcoholics, but that list is not for you."

Those were the thoughts that ODAP constantly put into my mind. Being new in A.A., at that time, I had no inclination to record any names. My crafty alcoholic practice of omission was still alive, and stayed alive, until I followed the advice of an older member, and made up my list. It wasn't too hard to do once I became submissive enough to realize the need for compliance with this step. It was really an adjunct to contentment in living a life without alcohol.

Step Nine was difficult for me to carry out, but it was made to order for ODAP. He had ready objections to making any restitutions to the people my drinking had injured. So, naturally, he was not worried about the injury it might cause them if I did try to make restitutions. His advice was definite and to the point.

"Don't complicate your effort to carry out this step by calling upon a lot of individuals. They are not interested in you, so stay away from them. They would only ridicule you, and perhaps kick you out of their homes, if you did call."

"You are the only one to whom amends can be made, and you make them by showing your old friends that you can drink with them like any normal person."

"Be a man, show the world that you can handle your liquor without getting into trouble. A.A. says you can't. You show them you can."

"Thousands of social drinkers have no trouble. Drink, if you wish to, *but observe this one precaution — never drink the morning after*. You'll be safe if you follow this simple advice."

ODAP knows all the mental gimmicks that disrupt contented sobriety for A.A. newcomers. This was quite evident when I considered making amends to my family.

41

"It's not wise to get too concerned about them," he cautioned me. "Remember how they kept you in the doghouse during your drinking years? You are sober now, what more can they ask for? Do they expect perfection?"

"The Big Book says; You shouldn't dodge your creditors. Don't get carried away with that idea. Pass them all up. Let them wait for their money. You have more important problems to contend with."

Today, Odap's dishonest rationalization is apparent. But from my own experience, I can fully sympathize with the newcomer who is still pledged by his misleading advice.

It was an aggravating period in my life, a period in which I was belligerent and unhappy much of the time.

That sinful little monkey rode my shoulder day and night, always interfering with my inclinations to live the Twelve Steps as successful A.A. members lived them.

He was viciously intolerant of Step Ten. "What now?" he grumbled in sharp antagonistic tones. "More inventories? Will they never end?"

"Who is kidding who? You made an inventory in Step Four. You listed names in Step Eight, and considered making amends in Step Nine. Must you become an A.A. accountant to succeed in this program?"

"How come Step Ten has to drag out the action so long? Aren't you becoming rather sanctimonious by admitting your mistakes to everybody?"

"It seems that you are trying to out-clergy the clergymen. Few of them adhere to such strict regimentation as Step Ten demands from you."

At times, I shared ODAP's aversion to the daily practice of Step Ten. The suggestions in this step seemed too hard to follow. My attempts to follow them were far from perfect. Even so, whenever I tried, they rewarded me with feelings of partial accomplishment and a sense of well-being.

There is an old A.A. adage which tells us that we either progress or that we retrogress in living our program. Some members learn this the hard way. Other members follow Step Ten's suggestions and thus retain their sobriety.

At first, I carried a middle of the road attitude which made me question the advisability of total adherence to any of the Twelve Steps. This half-hearted effort divorced me from alcohol, but made me irritable and unhappy.

Although my attitude did not directly oppose the practice of Step Eleven, it did lack sufficient stimulus for deep reflection upon God's will, or the way in which I was to carry it out. My habit of living upon self-will was too well established to submit to His will without a struggle.

An alcoholic's decisions are most inconsistent. He can accept and reject a decision almost instantaneously. He decides to stop drinking, throws away his bottle, and in five minutes he calls the liquor store for another bottle. A.A. used my inconsistencies for a better purpose, which was the case with Step Eleven.

My opposition to Step Eleven was overcome by thoughts of my helplessness and desperation before A.A. I discussed this with my sponsor, who advised me to continue praying many times each day. My first attempts were feeble, but they got me started upon a daily spiritual procedure, which I believe was the difference between success and failure.

There was no delayed action after I gave Step Eleven a fair trial. It was truly a stimulating experience. Over-night, my whole concept of life started to change for the better. It gave me a zest for living, honestly and unselfishly, which I had never had before. It filled my mind with a desire for future sobriety and service to all alcoholics.

Surely, these were worthy motives, but since they were based upon single experiences they were misleading. I assumed they would always stay with me. I soon learned that they were not my permanent possession, but that they must be renewed daily.

ODAP, who had been hiding in the shadow of my insane behavior for so many years, knew my weakness and my inconsistency to carry out a good intention. So he waited for an opportune time to intercept my Eleventh Step efforts. He didn't have to wait long. He seized upon daily meditation as the weapon with which to deter my well-intended advance toward successful application of this step. He presented facts and logic with which my confused mind could not always cope.

The Big Book suggested that upon awakening I plan the twenty-four hours ahead. That I ask God to keep my mental faculties free from self-pity, dishonesty or self-seeking motives. That I have my wife or friends join me in morning meditation, and at night to constructively review the day, asking God's forgiveness for my errors.

My work required written reports each day, and they were never completed before midnight. At seven o'clock the next morning I started getting ready for work again. As a result, I was not too alert mentally in the morning, and ODAP capitalized upon this condition.

"Why don't you put off this early morning prayer business until noon?" he asked. "You'll be able to do it then and you can kill two birds with one stone by reviewing your day and at the same time asking God's forgiveness for your errors."

"Forget about having your wife or friends join you in silent meditation. That's impossible! You travel and live in hotels where the guests would think you were off your rocker if you did such things in public."

"What about God's will? Did he ever get you any big business accounts, or did you get them yourself by drinking with your customers? You'd better give this matter some thought. Your A.A. principles could easily lose business for you."

"Be realistic. Is it possible your personality could have changed so much in a few months, or are you kidding yourself?"

"Wouldn't it be better for your business if you paid more attention to it, rather than devoting so much time to A.A.?"

ODAP never quits. These thoughts must have come from him. Certainly they did not come from the God I understood. The God who had provided me contented sobriety, up until that time. So I prayed to Him to protect me from ODAP's evil influence. My prayer was answered each day. This brought me real peace of mind, and sustained my desire to help other alcoholics as suggested in Step Twelve.

Step Twelve, I found, was most specific, and precisely formulated. First it stipulated a con-

47

dition under which it would work, and then, it suggested the work to be done. In fact, it seemed to embrace most all of the Twelve Step program.

Step Twelve predicts real spiritual attainment for members who live the A.A. program. It suggests that we work with other alcoholics, and continue a spiritual way of life in all of our daily activities.

For the newcomer in A.A. there is so much to learn, and do, that full acceptance of Step Twelve seems impossible. To be quite factual, it is hard to practice in the beginning.

This does not mean, of course, that a new member cannot benefit from the practice of Step Twelve, or share his sobriety with an alcoholic who calls for help, providing he wishes to do so. He should use every available A.A. opportunity to gain as much experience as possible. If he is quite new in A.A., he will be wise to make the call with an older member.

Being spiritually awakened (even though it be a slight awakening) opens the door for us to a happier sober life. Through it we are given faith that God will use us as instruments to carry out His will. Our job is to be willing and ready to accept the opportunities as they present themselves to us.

He does not promise to remove all of our problems, but when we put our trust in Him, He does make possible a harmonious way to either overcome them, or to avoid them.

God does not force us to live the Twelve Steps, He simply grants us sobriety if we are consistent in their daily practice. If failure results it is because we will not yield to their simple requirements, or because we will not make an honest admission of our alcoholic addiction to ourselves.

Fear, dishonesty, resentment and reservations are a few of the mental blocks which impede our progress in the A.A. way of life. These emotions often cause us to drink again.

ODAP knows this. He is well aware of these weak spots in our character, and he always selects the proper time to weaken our defense against them.

Always in opposition to better achievement of our Twelve Step objectives, his ironic logic can temporarily delay, and sometimes prevent, much needed contemplation of necessary

49

A.A. action. Step Twelve presents a favorite field of malicious sabotage for him.

"What do you know about spiritual awakening? Aren't you just using an expression which you heard in A.A.", he asked me.

"The only spirits you are familiar with are those you got from alcohol and they put you to sleep, they didn't awaken you. Remember?"

"If you are so spiritual minded, why do you still pad your expense account? I don't blame you though. Your company doesn't pay you enough money to live on."

ODAP resorted to every possible trick to thwart my attempts of sponsorship. He preyed upon my desire for anonymity as an excuse for avoiding an experience which our Big Book says, "We must not miss."

Using his deceptive reasoning as justification for bypassing sponsorship, he offered the following mental escape devices to my credulous, unsuspecting mind.

"Aren't you falling for a lot of A.A. double talk?" he asked me. "They lead you to believe that your identity will be protected—then they ask you to call upon prospective members, and expose it."

"What about this idea of Carrying the Message to a lot of drunks you've never heard of before? How are you going to stay anonymous doing that?"

"Have you no concern for the reputation of your family? What will your neighbors think when they learn you are an alcoholic?"

"You'd better watch out calling on these drunks at all hours of the day and night—some of them live in pretty tough neighborhoods. You might end up with a cracked skull some night."

"A lot of these would-be members are not going to stay sober. They'll only get you into family quarrels and make you an easy touch for financial help."

"Let some other member help them. You've got your sobriety. It's up to them to take care of themselves. Are you trying to qualify for the role of Good Samaritan? Let the older members take that role."

"Some members say that A.A. is a selfish program. You've got yourself to look after. Why

51

spoil your own chances wet-nursing a lot of drunken strangers?"

"As for practicing the Twelve Step principles in all your affairs, it can't be done, so why wear yourself out trying to achieve such an improbable undertaking?"

That crook ODAP, just deals in half truths. None of us can be perfect, we only work toward perfection, but our small efforts, if sincere, are sufficient to keep us sober.

He has given some members the opinion that our Twelve Step program is a selfish program. If living a contented, sober life in which we help other alcoholics to escape insanity and alcoholic death is selfish, then the meaning of the word has been changed without Webster's knowledge.

Webster's current definition of selfish is: "Caring unduly for oneself, regarding one's comfort at the expense of that of others." So here again, ODAP gives us a half-truth.

It seemed that every time I took a step up the A.A. ladder ODAP tried to kick it out from under me.

He is the Devil's chief advocate and he keeps

the pressure on all A.A. members Twenty-Four Hours a day. We are never free from it.

Every move we make in the right direction — ODAP stands ready to throw his monkey wrench into our A.A. machinery.

Our problem is that we don't recognize these monkey wrenches, for they don't resemble monkey wrenches.

He inflicts us with mental drunkenness which comes in the form of fear, anger, dishonesty, resentment, jealousy, hatred and mental or physical exhaustion.

It's a smooth, tricky approach, but ODAP often makes it work. When we find a member indulging too heavily in any type of mental drunkenness, we know his sobriety is at stake.

Now, I've mentioned just a few of the ways in which ODAP throws up road-blocks to hinder our recovery from alcoholism.

There are many other ways in which he uses emotions from OUR DEVILISH ALCOHOLIC PERSONALITIES TO DRIVE US BACK TO THE BOTTLE.

He conjures up all sorts of excuses to keep us

53

from reading THE BIG BOOK, and to keep us from A.A. meetings.

These are both very serious matters, for when we find enough excuses that we consider legitimate, to stop reading the book, and to keep us away from meetings—we are in real trouble.

Alcoholics form bad habits easily, and we quickly form the habit of not reading the book, or coming to meetings at all.

ODAP plays upon all our weaknesses. He eggs us on to gossip and fault finding, or other harmful things, which will spread dissension in an A.A. group.

His strategy is to keep us on dry drunks. For he knows that a member who is mentally drunk has the bad habit of getting physically drunk, and quite often, of dropping out of A.A.

The Big Book assures us that our sobriety depends upon the daily help we receive from a Higher power. ODAP prompts us to ignore this fact and to depend upon self-will instead.

SELF-WILL. Under the spiritual inspiration and guidance afforded us as we practice the

54

Twelve Steps, will power becomes a source of constructive energy in a member's life. Without this spiritual help, however, self-will takes over and becomes a short cut to renewed drunkenness.

ODAP fills us with self-pity and resentment over the assumption that we are not getting enough recognition for our work, and efforts in A.A.

He tries to convince us that we are not appreciated enough at home for the great sacrifices we are making to keep sober.

At times, he convinces some members that they have really mastered the A.A. program, that graduation is at hand, and in this manner he gets these members out of A.A., only to start drinking again.

Thanks to God, who is the Higher Power in A.A., there is a much brighter picture than that devilish monkey ODAP allows his followers to see.

In fact, his followers are but a small minority compared to the thousands of successful members in our wonderful fellowship.

All of us in A.A. are subject to harmful urges

and temptations, but for the members who study the Big Book, who become honest with themselves and try to follow the path of our Founders, *the miracle of A.A. is at work*.

It's at work in spite of ODAP's best efforts to stop it. ODAP still clings to our shoulders and whispers dishonest thoughts into our ears. But by this time he has lost much of his hypnotic power.

The Twelve Steps have taught us a daily way of life with which we can combat our harmful emotions and devote the strength of our minds to attaining happy, contented sobriety.

For the purposes of identification and comparison, I have used the analogy of two opposite powers in the A.A. fellowship to emphasize the help of a Higher Power, and the barriers which Odap builds up to obstruct our efforts to live a normal, sober life.

Successful members soon learn to recognize these barriers as they study the book, "Alcoholics Anonymous," and try to live the Twelve Steps, as thousands of sober members have done since the inception of A.A.

These are the same barriers which unsuccessful members are either ignorant of, or too full of self-centered interests to try to correct.

This brings us to a cross-road in our recovery progress. From here on, we either "sink or swim," for God as we understand Him, now gives us a choice in the matter.

Our decision is a crucial decision at this point. We can either drink ourselves into alcoholic oblivion, or we can acquire happy, sober lives in A.A.

We will have problems — many problems, but through belief in God, and the practice of our A.A. principles we will sublimate these problems, which might, otherwise, send us back into the slavery of alcoholism.

We are still alcoholics. Sometimes, we get grandiose ideas, and by sheer will-power we attempt to combat our problems singlehanded.

This is a bad practice, for experience has taught us that will-power is a tricky, unreliable source of help for alcoholics. A.A. recommends that we try a daily practice of the Twelve Steps instead.

That is the way we find our strength. For by their practice, we can eventually overcome the

many urges and emotions which stand between us and contented sobriety.

Even so, let us always keep in mind this simple
A.A. paradox: by daily practice of our Twelve
Step program, we are never in real danger of
drinking. But with that dishonest little monkey
ODAP around, we are never entirely safe.

The Alcoholic Paradox

By Austin Ripley

The alcoholic, of course, is many things, as we all know. He is the world's supreme paradox. He drinks, not because he would, but because he must.

He does not drink for pleasure, he drinks to pain, yet he drinks. He will mortgage the wealth of the future to pay off the debts of the past so that he may drink up the non-existent present.

He is the only one in nature, I think, who seeks stimulation in a sedative, only to find that it acts upon his nerves as excited misery.

He seeks to inflate his puny little ego in the provocative wine of Bacchus and succeeds in shriveling his soul in the bitter gall of remorse.

He escapes desperately to free himself from the facts of reality and runs headlong into the prison of fantasy. Success is just as fatal as failure to the alcoholic.

He will drink with exhilaration to success and to sadness and misfortune. He drinks to get high in the evening, knowing how low he will be in the morning. When the alcoholic smilingly gets to the first drink he can get, he is transported to heaven and when he is unable to get the last drink he can pour, he is transported to hell.

The alcoholic, like most people, thrills to the beauty of life and then how frequently he seeks the ugliness in existence.

When he is sober he craves to be drunk. When he is drunk he prays to be sober.

Such is the weird paradox of the alcoholic, that the only way in which he can feel better is to drink that which makes him feel worse. He starts out on his drinking, no matter who he is, with all the dignity of a king, and winds up his drinking like a clown.

So he goes his incredible, incomprehensible, paradoxical way, leaving in his wake his human wreckage, that which he does cherish most. Down the road of alcoholic oblivion he stumbles and staggers, until he either finds himself at the door of A.A. and the halfway house, or death intercedes.

The Quietest Room in Town

By Bill Kiley with permission from the January 1958 Reader's Digest. Copyright 1957 by The Reader's Digest Assn., Inc. Condensed from Los Angeles Mirror-news.

They are ready for you. They expect you. You will never know about it, so I'll fill in the details for you.

The beginning for you will be when you stagger happily to your car. The beginning for them will be when the police radio tells the place where you piled up your car.

You won't hear the sirens coming. The ambulance and the police car will arrive together. They will check you over, then pronounce you dead.

A few curious people will stop and gaze at your torn, bloody remains. Some of them will get sick.

The ambulance driver will roll out a leather covered stretcher. The attendant will stuff your hands up under your belt — then grab you under the arms, and the driver will take your legs. After they place you upon the stretcher, you will be covered with a sheet.

They will drive you to the coroner's office, and there a deputy coroner will wheel you to a big scale. He will remove the sheet. You will be weighed and measured. He will make a note of any scars or other marks.

He will cover you again, and take you to a small white room to give you a bath, because they have hoses in that room, and traffic victims are always bloody. They will clean you and embalm you.

Next, you will be moved into a long hall with many stretchers lined up against its pale green walls. There are forty one crypts. If things are dull, you will have a stretcher and a crypt all to yourself. But later you'll probably have company.

In an hour, or so, they will come back and move you again. This time they will take away the white sheet, and cover you with a blanket. You will be placed behind a huge enclosed glass window, so someone can look at you — like your wife, your husband or your parents, for someone must identify you. Don't worry though you won't be able to hear their cries.

Yes — they are waiting for you. The police, the ambulance crews, and the coroners down at the morgue. The morticians are expecting you.

So remember this as you toss down that last drink and climb behind the steering wheel of your car.

LANDMARKS IN A.A. HISTORY

1934 Summer: Dr. William D. Silkworth pronounces Bill W. hopeless.

1934 November: Bill's friend Ebby T. visits him, describes how he sobered up on spiritual principles.

1934 December: Bill's spiritual experience in Towns Hospital.

1935 Mother's Day: Doctor Bob and Bill meet in Akron, Ohio.

1935 June 10: Doctor Bob has his last drink; Alcoholics Anonymous founded.

1937 November: 40 cases sober; first realization of certain success.

1938 May: The Alcoholic Foundation established as a trusteeship for A.A.

1938 December: The Twelve Steps were written.

1939 April: The "Big Book" Alcoholics Anonymous was published.

1939 August: Doctor Bob and Sister Ignatia

start work at St. Thomas Hospital, Akron, Ohio; treat 5,000 in 10 years.

1940 February: First A.A. world service office opened on Vesey Street in New York City.

1940 Father Dowling and Doctor Fosdick, first of many religious leaders to endorse A.A.

1941 March: Saturday Evening Post article jumps membership from 2,000 to 8,000.

1944 June: First A.A. Grapevine.

1945 Doctor Silkworth and Teddy R. begin work at Knickerbocker Hospital in New York; they treat 10,000 alcoholics in 10 years.

1946 Twelve Traditions formulated, and first published in Grapevine.

1949 Medical associations hail Alcoholics Anonymous.

1950 June: First International A.A. Convention, Cleveland, Ohio. Traditions adopted.

1950 November: Doctor Bob's death.

1951 April: Doctor Silkworth's death.

1951 April: First General Service Conference.

1951 October: Lasker Award given to A.A. by the American Public Health Association.

1953 June: The book, Twelve Steps and Twelve Traditions published.

1955 July: Twentieth Anniversary Convention, St. Louis Missouri; The three legacies: Recovery, Unity and Service were given to the safe-keeping of the movement.

1957 The book, A.A. Comes of Age, was published.

1960 July: Twenty-Fifth Anniversary Convention, Long Beach, California.

1965 July: Thirtieth Anniversary Convention, Toronto, Canada.

1970 July: Thirty Fifth Anniversary Convention, Miami, Florida.

Alcohol

Facts and Misconceptions About its Effects Upon Alcoholics

Medical science, organized religion and Alcoholics Anonymous all contribute to rehabilitating the alcoholic, but with some variation regarding their methods of treatment.

The alcoholic who drinks is not particularly interested in receiving help from any source, except the bottle. Either through ignorance of the harmful effects of alcohol upon his mind and body, or his unwillingness to stop drinking, he rejects all plans that would separate him from alcohol.

The following points may help enlighten us about the beverage use of alcohol, and remove many misconceptions about its use.

1. The drinking alcoholic considers all intoxicating drinks as beverages. He cannot visualize them as harmful, or poisonous to himself.

2. Knowledgeable, recovered alcoholics agree that such drinks may be beverages

for people who can control them. For themselves, they consider alcohol to be a liquid narcotic which depresses their nerve centers, and incites them to idiotic and unpredictable behavior.

3. Some religious organizations label the alcoholic a sinner, and attempt to solve his drinking problem by saving his soul, but with little success.

4. Most medical doctors disregard the sinful aspect of alcoholism, and treat it quite successfully upon the basis of physical and mental illness, but willingly turn over their patients to Alcoholics Anonymous for continued recovery.

5. Alcoholics indulge in alcohol to promote their social and business status: to prevent illness, to relieve tension, and to end frustration. These are some of the reasons which they offer to excuse their drinking. Under close scrutiny, however, their reasons turn out to be nothing but excuses.

6. Is alcohol a food? It is a food with extremely limited nutritional value. It contains few proteins, carbohydrates, miner-

als, vitamins or other body building qualities.

7. Does alcohol stimulate our thinking and physical activities? At first, it seems that way. It really has a depressive effect upon our nervous systems, which becomes quite apparent in habitual usage. It then irritates us and causes discomfort.

8. Does alcohol improve our alertness, our physical skill and endurance? No, it retards them.

9. Does the use of alcoholic beverages cause crime in our society? Not in all cases, yet their use is responsible for many crimes.

10. Is alcoholism a community health problem? Yes; it is only exceeded by heart disease, cancer and mental illness. It would rank first, if we considered the ill health and suffering it brings to the alcoholic and his family.

11. Can clergymen help our A.A. Fellowship? Yes, enlightened clergymen send us prospective members. Their help is also needed by members in taking step five.

New Slants on Old Ideas

Peace of mind and drunkenness are incompatible for the drinking alcoholic. Contented sobriety is a Twelve Step miracle which many members acquire.

It does not come without effort. They only achieve it through honest self-analysis, spiritual help, right thinking and loss of self-centeredness. And then willingness to share their miracle with other alcoholics.

Every member will be buffeted by waves of hard luck as long as he depends upon his own selfish ambitions. His efforts at self-control fail to keep him sober.

Although he is helpless at times, he is never hopeless in A.A. for when he earnestly applies himself to correcting his character defects, he will be rewarded with both health and sobriety.

A.A. members do not always get what they want in life. No member gets all he wishes or prays for. He gets exactly what he earns.

His fondest wishes and most intense prayers are gratified only when they are in harmony with his daily thoughts and his constructive A.A. actions.

＝彩＝

"Where there is a will there is a way." How true this is with drinking alcoholics. Nothing else matters when they start drinking. Time, fortune and reputation are of little consideration as they appease their irresistible compulsion to get tight.

＝彩＝

Step Eleven suggests "prayer and meditation." It is the best policy for our members. IT WORKS. Let none of us forget to remember that the steps we forget to work cannot possibly do us any good. Then, while we are at it, let's remember the desperation that brought us into A.A. in the first place. It's so easy to forget you know.

＝彩＝

The egocentric alcoholic is tempted to dwell upon the big shot, he assumed himself to be in the past. He loves to hold onto this thought. It should be avoided as it robs him of humility.

Let us stop harassing our minds about the

71

past. Let's Live Today. Let's capitalize upon present opportunities. Let's start in deflating our over inflated egos. Perhaps you may find this bit of verse helpful.

It may be that some years ago you had plenty of Long Green. But they don't count for much, you know, the good times you have seen.

You can't run this years motor car on last years gasoline. So look forward. Lose yourself in A.A. efforts. You've wasted too much time already.

The Big Book says we live on "A Daily Reprieve which is contingent upon our Spiritual Condition." Thus we acquire *inactive alcoholic personalities*.

There is a caution to be observed, however, as we are just one drink away from a drunk and that one shot of liquor in any form, could reactivate our dormant personalities and return us to the insanity of alcoholism.

By nature, alcoholics are high-strung, impetuous people. They forget how to be quiet and too often lose the art of silent meditation.

They then forget that God is more powerful than themselves and that He can send His enabling power to work through them.

They forget that He can project His voice to them, if they will listen. They are never free from fear and anxiety until they listen to Him say," BE STILL AND KNOW THAT I AM GOD."

Bible interpretation is not my forte, but I always wonder if St. Matthew wasn't referring to an alcoholic when he said, "When the unclean spirit has gone out of a man, he walketh through dry places, seeking rest and findeth none.

"Then he said, I will return to my house from whence I came out, and when he is come, he findeth it empty, swept, and garnished.

"Then goeth he, and taketh with him seven other spirits more wicked than himself, and they enter in and dwell there, and the last state of that man is worse than the first."

Paraphrasing some of James Allen's brilliant comments it seems that an alcoholic is made

73

or unmade by himself. Through his compulsive drinking he forges the tools with which he destroys himself.

A.A. provides him the Twelve Step tools with which he can build for himself health, happiness and contented sobriety.

By the right choice and intelligent application of these tools an alcoholic can ascend to a high level of a sober useful life.

But, by the wrong use of these tools, he descends below the level of the beast. It is between these two extremes of living that each member makes or breaks himself.

"Act is the blossom of thought, and joy and suffering are its fruits. Thus does an A.A. member garner in the sweet and bitter fruitage of his own husbandry." How true this is in A.A.

In A.A. members are anxious to improve their wealth and social position, but at times unwilling to improve themselves therefore they remain bound in mental drunkenness.

A member's circumstances may be hard and

seem impossible. His friends may be uncongenial, but this condition will not last long if he will become honest and make the Twelve Steps his daily way of life.

We cannot help a newcomer in A.A. unless the newcomer is willing to be helped. And even then he must develop his own strength. He can profit from our example, but he must correct his own errors to succeed in A.A.

Although the book, Alcoholics Anonymous deals with the serious aspects of recovery from alcoholism, it also suggests that we do not take ourselves too seriously.

In "The Family Afterwards," paragraph thirty two suggests that we include humor, fun and laughter in our A.A. way of life, otherwise we could never attract new members. For example, the following story was heard at a recent A.A. meeting.

A drunk stood before a court judge. The judge said; "You were arrested for being drunk and setting a hotel bed on fire. What have you got to say for yourself?"

"It's a damn lie judge," yelled the prisoner, "The bed was on fire when I got into it."

75

False pride is a great burden to some of us. Hence, the importance of a member's right attitude in his attempt to recover from alcoholism.

This applies to the newcomer, particularly. Newcomers are wise to realize that they can do A.A. little good at first, but that A.A. can save their lives.

They should never join A.A. just for the benefit of their wives, their children or their employers. They should join A.A. because they are ill. They are the ones who will benefit.

They should face the fact that if they die, the wife can marry a better man. The kids will then have a better father and their employers can replace them with a better employee.

With these hard facts in mind, the newcomer stands a better chance of succeeding with his new way of life than if he feels he is doing someone a favor by being in A.A.

THE LORD'S PRAYER

OUR FATHER, WHICH ART IN HEAVEN, HALLOWED BE THY NAME. THY KINGDOM COME. THY WILL BE DONE, IN EARTH AS IT IS IN HEAVEN. GIVE US THIS DAY OUR DAILY BREAD, AND FORGIVE US OUR TRESPASSES, AS WE FORGIVE THEM THAT TRESPASS AGAINST US, AND LEAD US NOT INTO TEMPTATION; BUT DELIVER US FROM EVIL; FOR THINE IS THE KINGDOM, THE POWER, AND THE GLORY, FOR EVER AND EVER.

AMEN.

ONE ALCOHOLIC'S VERSION OF THE LORD'S PRAYER

Believers in a Higher Power? Agnostics? Atheists? Under which category do you fall? Categories are unimportant providing you are an alcoholic and are desperate enough to live the A.A. program to stop drinking.

Newcomers sometimes erroneously assume that the Alcoholics Anonymous fellowship is a religious organization because several of the Twelve Steps contain spiritual suggestions. This, of course, is a false assumption.

Some of the steps are of a spiritual nature, but they require no religious involvements: no creeds, no dogmas or doctrines. A.A. demands nothing from its members. The only requirement for membership is that the applicant be an alcoholic.

Although The Lord's Prayer is recited by many groups at the close of their meetings, it is not universally accepted by all groups for that purpose. Since it is used by some groups, perhaps one member's opinion of the prayer might be of interest.

A fellowship as large as Alcoholics Anonymous naturally has members of many faiths, some of which are not compatible in their religious beliefs. But regardless of their individual beliefs, A.A. brings its members together upon the common ground of faith in a Higher Power. The vital need of spiritual help is not a secret to anyone. It is the motivating factor of success in our fellowship.

Intelligent alcoholic agnostics and atheists soon learn the need of God's help if they are to succeed in their new way of life. It takes no master-mind to realize that without His help there could be no A.A., and without A.A. help that they would shortly revert to the insanity of alcoholism, or at the best, become a group of unhappy, sick people on perpetual dry-drunks.

There are no atheists among successful A.A. members. A few of us may have denied God in the beginning, but not anymore. Many of us learned the hard way, but we now know that sobriety demands surrender of old, rebellious thoughts, and to keep sober we must believe in a Power greater than ourselves.

QUESTION? Just how do we regard The

Lord's Prayer? Do we simply give it lip-service without any serious contemplation about its intended meaning? Have we recited it so often that we hurriedly mouth its words like a group of trained parrots?

The answers to these questions are important, and worthy of our consideration. They are questions each of us can answer by separating the prayer into eight divisions, and then studying them. The first division starts with these two words: "OUR FATHER."

"OUR FATHER"

A human father is a male person who has begotten a child. He can be of any race, and he comes in all colors, and in various shades. He is subject to many emotions, and to all human illness, *including alcoholism*.

Undoubtedly, the reference to Our Father in The Lord's Prayer is directed to a spiritual father, rather than a paternal one. Children, at an early age, understand this, but a few contentious-minded alcoholics find it hard to accept, or to try to understand. Why they react this way is probably because they have had more experience lousing-up simple matters than anyone else.

To become a competent alcoholic louser-upper requires long years of intensive daily training. To qualify for this questionable title one must constantly poach upon the love and charity of both friends and relatives, day after day.

During this period of poaching the alcoholic deteriorates mentally, and divorces himself from God until he becomes a spiritual orphan. This causes him to be dishonest, and extremely self-centered. If he prays at all he uses the term *MY FATHER rather than "OUR FATHER,"* as suggested in The Lord's Prayer.

Today, A.A. offers all alcoholics a second chance to rebuild their lives. Therefore, it seems, that the time has come, for those of us who are members, to stop playing God, and to stop making a farce of our participation in The Lord's Prayer.

So, as we pray, and say "Our Father," let us remember that we are talking to God who is a loving Father. Let us, also, remember that He has many children who are our brothers, and that as He loved us, we in turn, should offer love, service and sobriety to each other.

81

"WHICH ART IN HEAVEN"

The A.A. fellowship is established upon the principles of love and service. The Twelve Steps are not connected with organized religion, but they do mention God, and stress the importance of a spiritual awakening to a member's sobriety.

Because many members use The Lord's Prayer as a helpful adjunct to their spiritual development, it seems in order for one member to express his views on this matter, *as heaven has different meanings to different people.*

Drinking alcoholics waste no time visualizing Heaven. Heaven, for them, is a life of unrestricted alcoholic indulgence, with ample financial funds, and no hangovers or worry of any kind.

Some alcoholics enjoy a real pleasurable existence drinking unbelievable amounts of alcohol for awhile. Later, they learn that life is made up of many opposite conditions, like heat and cold, like day and night, *like normal drinkers and alcoholics.*

By the time these facts have penetrated their

befuddled minds their drinking joys have left them, and have been converted into an alcoholic hell on earth. Sometimes the victims drink themselves to death. Some of them escape death, but become quite ill before desperation brings them into A.A. Arrested alcoholics know a lot about the drinking hell they have experienced here on earth. Like other people, of course, they have had no actual experience with heaven.

Webster defines hell as a place of punishment for sinful people after death. Father Edward Dowling, a Jesuit priest, and a staunch friend of Alcoholics Anonymous, once said: "If I ever get to heaven it will be from running away from hell."

The exact way to heaven is still a mystery. In A.A. we believe that God is the key to our sobriety, and for an alcoholic, sobriety is his present heaven on earth. Traits of love, service and forgiveness are said to be attributes of God. Perhaps as we develop them we are being drawn closer to both God, and heaven. We hope so, but of course, no one can be sure.

Many of us are willing to concede to such

reasoning, but we do not wish to surrender our selfish lives to God's dictates. We lose Him quite often, but He is not lost. He always comes to us when we search for Him.

Pride often blocks our willingness to ask His Help. We feel that we must handle our own affairs, and that He might stunt our personal efforts in that direction.

What we actually need is to pray for spiritual help and direction to do God's will each day. That will help us as true prayer creates a willingness in us to be directed along the right spiritual paths.

Prayers of appreciation are indispensable to happy sobriety in the A.A. fellowship. They kill our reservation, they keep us open-minded, and they increase our faith in the help of available spiritual power.

Our sobriety does not depend upon the little we can do for God. He manages to get along very well in spite of us. Our welfare is dependent upon what we believe He can do for us, and in asking Him to do it. Lack of faith and prayer prevents Him from helping us.

God can only express Himself in, and through us, so let us remember that although we are sons of God, that we are only sons, not kings. Our job is to do His will. His job is to give us the power to carry it out. That is the reason why we pray; "OUR FATHER WHICH ART IN HEAVEN."

"HALLOWED BE THY NAME"

Taken out of context, these four words, "Hallowed Be Thy Name," would have little meaning, even to those who say The Lord's Prayer. Few alcoholics will take the time to study the significance of those four words.

The words "Bottled in Bond" were familiar to us, but the word Hallowed was not to be found in our drinking vocabularies. We frequented many bars, and other drinking establishments, where the management extended us credit and friendship, but we never considered these places as holy, or hallowed. God was often spoken of in profanity, yet The Lord's Prayer was seldom, if ever recited.

From the barroom to Alcoholics Anonymous is a drastic change for all of us. Alcoholics are not in A.A. long before they are faced with Step Two. This is a great shock to our conceited minds, for Step Two questions our sanity. It recommends that we had better believe in some power greater than alcohol to restore us to sane behavior.

As we maintain our sobriety and our sanity starts returning, we can show a little reverence to God by thanking Him for the part He played in keeping us out of the Booby Hatch. It would hardly be reverence unless we offered it in prayer.

The old English meaning of the word "hallowed" associates it with, holy, whole-sacred and divine. Sincere members will not haggle about God's hallowed position. To stay sober, and happy, they will surrender their wills to Him in appreciation of His great power to prolong their sobriety.

In due time, knowledgeable members will make their decisions to live the Twelve Steps and thus establish their fellowship with God, which will bring them a better understanding of why we pray: "Hallowed Be Thy Name."

"THY KINGDOM COME, THY WILL BE DONE IN EARTH AS IT IS IN HEAVEN"

Surely none of our finite minds are capable of

fully knowing God's mind, either in earth or in heaven. Luckily for us, He does not expect us to advance beyond our limited mental capabilities. We should, however, be open-minded and try to understand this part of The Lord's prayer.

"Thy Kingdom Come" is not easy to understand, or to keep simple. Although it is apart from things we are not familiar with, we can intuitively arrive at its meaning for us, simply through prayer.

Contemplation upon these three words raises three questions which fill us with uncertainty and fear. *One*: Do we really want God's kingdom to come? *Two*: How soon do we want it to come? *Three*: Can an alcoholic belong to His kingdom?

Do these three words impose an obligation upon us to help develop God's kingdom upon earth? It has been said that, "He has a plan for everyone and that He has a plan for us." These are most interesting thoughts to ponder. Do they challenge our spiritual beliefs? They seem to confuse many people.

Step Twelve in our program indicates that we have a definite plan to carry out, and when

87

properly acted upon it serves to develop our conscience — thus inspiring us to more purposeful achievements in our daily lives.

Thousands of alcoholics have discovered this plan and have proved its effectiveness to help themselves and to help others. Once we put the plan into action, God seems to open all doors, and to remove all obstacles that would obstruct our efforts to remain sober.

It is helpful to meditate upon this fact, for we know it is true, as we have seen it materialize in the lives of numerous alcoholics whom we have sponsored. Furthermore, we have seen them carry their message to other helpless alcoholics. Could this indicate it was done because of spiritual inspiration, and not for any self-centered reasons? Yes, we think so.

On the other hand, we have seen many alcoholics fail for lack of spiritual beliefs. This alerts us to the fact that without God's help, no alcoholic will submit to a spiritual plan which requires abstinence from alcohol.

The Big Book, "Alcoholics Anonymous" refers to the drinking alcoholic as a person who casts himself into disaster because of his self-centered drinking obsession. Even after months, or years of sobriety he finds it hard to govern self-will.

Alcoholics who choose to be guided only by their own will-power live dangerous, haphazard lives, ruled mostly by negative thinking. Refusing to learn from previous experience, they are only heading for more trouble.

Too much negative thinking will foster mental attitudes that bring on "stinking thinking," and minds bogged down with such thoughts invariably not only make us unhappy, but head us back to the bottle. It's a slow process, but that's how it works.

How we work it is a matter of choice. We can settle for "God's will be done in earth as it is in heaven," or our will to be done as we see fit. It is a grave matter about which we should give much consideration, as heretofore our will has resulted in alcoholism.

It is not easy for an alcoholic to practice the principles of the Twelve Steps, as our founders suggested they should be practiced. But, in doing so, we will, to the best of our ability, be conforming with God's will each day of our lives on earth. This probably falls far short of

His requirements in heaven, but it may head us in the right direction.

"GIVE US THIS DAY OUR DAILY BREAD"

In meditating upon Our Daily Bread, we might consider another affirmation which says: "Man shall not live by bread alone, but by every word that proceeds from the mouth of God." Even the most egotistical finds it hard to deny these statements.

Prior to A.A. we didn't eat much bread; there were more times we didn't eat anything. We tried to exist upon an alcoholic diet, but with little success. As a result we gradually suffered many metabolic changes because of alcoholic poisoning.

Our uncontrolled use of alcohol created both physical and mental problems. Mentally, we often reverted to emotional levels of thirteen-year-old youngsters. Our lives were truly unmanageable, but thanks to our present daily way of life those hectic experiences need no longer exist.

Because alcoholics are the children of a loving Father, we can expect that He will provide us with all our needs. To survive we have to have food, housing, clothing, free will, and helpful associations with other human beings. So when we pray for daily bread, it is reasonable to feel that these other things are included.

We come to look upon such needs as gifts from God. Actually, they are free gifts for the asking, but to get them we must pray for them, and that is an obstacle which often fools us. *We forget to pray.*

When our prayers are unselfish, and backed up with faith, God usually grants our requests. They are seldom permanent possessions, however, for they are ours only as long as we continue daily conscious contact with God.

Sometimes, we form the mistaken idea that simple recognition of God will bring us all of our heart's desires. This would be an easy, convenient method, if it worked. We soon learn that it isn't that easy, and that it doesn't work that way. We must earn everything we get from God by belief in His power to provide, and prayers of thanks for His provisions.

It would be wishful thinking to enter a bank and expect a cashier to cash a check unless we had money deposited in that bank. It seems just as far fetched to expect God's help unless we have made liberal deposits of faith and prayer in His spiritual bank.

The lifeblood of the A.A. fellowship is dependent upon the sobriety of its members and upon their willingness to share their experiences with other alcoholics. Such acts enlarge our spiritual bank accounts.

The newcomer needs help, and we give him help without any obligation. His only obligation is to himself. We show him the way, and explain that the rest is up to him; that he is the one who is alcoholic, and that we can not stay sober for him. We guide him, but he must do the work.

Accepting A.A.'s help and the Daily Bread referred to in The Lord's Prayer presents a problem. Bread spoils in a short time if not used. It has no value to sustain life unless we eat it. The Twelve Steps have no value either, unless we practice them each day.

Eating is such a personal matter that no person can do it for us. Food may be most plentiful, and all around us, yet we would soon die of starvation if we refused to eat. God's help is also all around us to be experienced personally, if we are to succeed in A.A.

Yesterday is gone. A.A.'s spiritual bread sufficed us for that day. It cannot be saved up for tomorrow. Members who try to hoard it get nowhere, as they are attempting the impossible. Ours is not a once a week program; to live successfully we should start anew each day.

Our Twelve Step program suggests that the art of living a sober life is in trying to perfect ourselves in each passing moment, and that our only hope for success tomorrow, is an attempt to live all of the Twelve Steps today.

"FORGIVE US OUR TRESPASSES AS WE FORGIVE THEM THAT TRESPASS AGAINST US."

To trespass is to go beyond the limits of what is considered right or moral. It implies an encroachment that breaks a law, or violates the rights of others. Drinking alcoholics are guilty of all these charges, and indebted to humanity because of them.

We all know this is true, but for an alcoholic to ask forgiveness of his trespasses is not in

93

keeping with his true nature, and he rebels against the idea. Such a concession requires an attitude of humility and submission, also a desire for freedom from pride and arrogance which very few alcoholics possess, or are they willing to indulge in.

At times our progress in A.A. slows down as we forget to forgive other people, and we balk at asking forgiveness of our many character defects; chief among which is RESENT-MENT.

RESENTMENT is a dangerous emotion for an alcoholic to become influenced by, as it temporarily separates him from God's help. Not only that, but it causes him to live apart from one of A.A.'s most fundamental principles, namely forgiveness.

Resentment in a member creates a sense of false power. It makes him live a self-regarding, personal existence without love or compassion for his fellow members. It provokes him to anger and makes him feel justified in injuring, or destroying, any thing or person he hates.

Few alcoholics escape this harmful emotion to which there seems to be no solution. Receptive, open-minded members will find a solution of their precarious predicament in the book, "Alcoholics Anonymous." The directions are given in Steps Eight and Nine. If you don't own this book, buy one and study it.

STEP EIGHT advises us to list the people whom our drinking has hurt and to acquire the willingness to recompense them for the injury. STEP NINE definitely proposes that we start this action at once: unless it would be harmful to the people involved.

JUSTIFIED RESENTMENT. Is there such a thing for us? If there is, it is not mentioned in the book, "Alcoholics Anonymous." That book warns us against all forms of resentment. It tells us that resentment is the major cause of all our troubles, and that it is a most ruinous emotion to happy sobriety.

CONDEMNATION. What about it? Evidently it is so closely related to resentment that we should avoid it, whenever possible. What about its brother, SELF-CONDEMNATION? How do we treat him? Treatment is not easy, but we accomplish it through prayer to *first forgive ourselves*. This works, but not

95

until after we have forgiven those who have harmed us.

FORGIVENESS. How do we acquire the capacity to become forgiving? The technique of forgiveness is quite simple. The only essential is our willingness to forgive. Once we really become willing, the hardest part of the battle is over.

Does this mean that our resentments can be quickly transformed into love for the people we have held in contempt for many years? No. It does not, but it does mean that members who try to live the A.A. program cannot afford to hate anybody.

It is unrealistic to believe that we can love everybody. Our Twelve Step program makes no such demand. It does suggest, however, that we treat every member with proper tolerance, and help him, if possible. It is our willingness to try this plan that tests the quality of our sobriety.

WHAT METHOD DO WE USE? How do we attain the willingness to forgive those who have offended us? The answer to these questions is not hard to arrive at, although many of us will not conform to its requirements after we find it.

The chapter on, "How it Works," in the book "Alcoholics Anonymous" answers these questions in great detail. The instructions will be less difficult to follow once we honestly admit our powerlessness over alcohol, and consider the hopelessness of our alcoholic lives.

The practice of forgiving can be started at night when we review the activities of the day, and in the morning when we ask God's guidance for that day. These are not the only opportunities, but they are the best.

Effective prayer and spiritual meditation are acts which we cannot accomplish in a hurry. They require time and mental concentration. They are easiest to perform when we are quiet and relaxed. They are most successful when we pray for the institutions, or persons we are at odds with.

Afterward, whenever resentful recollections of the offender, or the offence, disturb you — stop brooding about them. Remember that to keep brooding over such matters only makes you a slave to them. So pray about these things and then drop them from your mind.

Try this method of praying for awhile, and your resentment will give way to thoughts and acts of forgiveness. These thoughts, and acts, will bring you happiness, and at the same time protect your sobriety — day by day.

"LEAD US NOT INTO TEMPTATION BUT DELIVER US FROM EVIL"

This division of The Lord's Prayer can puzzle and completely confuse our members. If God is a loving father (which we believe Him to be) how can He possibly lead us into temptation? It seems most unreasonable to think He would do so.

It is only natural for us to question the correct sense or the true inner meaning implied. Since there are many perplexities involved here, let us first consider the sense of a newcomer in A.A. risking his sobriety by constantly frequenting bars because he loves their drinking atmosphere.

Is God leading him into temptation? Is that God's will for him? Surely God is not tempting him to hang out in such places. Does A.A. recommend his actions? What does our Big Book say about this? It says not to go except for a genuine reason and then only — if we are in good spiritual condition.

Under these circumstances, isn't the newcomer motivated by his own will when he exposes himself to any drinking environment? Has he forgotten that he became an alcoholic from drinking. Not from one drink, but from many drinks over many years? Alcoholics always find excuses for their behavior, but they can hardly blame God for their drinking.

The founders of A.A., as a result of their early experiences, were well aware of the subtle temptations, and the many drinking urges to which the future members of their fellowship would be subjected.

They knew that after a few months of spiritual development that the newcomer could become over-confident about his success and start substituting religion or other philosophies for the Twelve Steps. This still happens and we have a name for it. We call it "the free ride." Intelligent members soon learn that there is no free ride; that we must pay our fare daily, or get off of the A.A. plane.

Through meditation we become more conscious of the helpful influence of prayer to our sobriety, and to the need for better understanding and even closer contact with God. In fact, we gradually become more sensitive to the knowledge of what ethical and moral conduct we should follow.

An A.A. member should strive to reach this goal. It is a necessary phase of his development, but in no way, does it lessen his susceptibility to drinking urges, even some which he did not have before.

No member, at this stage of his development, will be tempted to rob a bank, or steal a case of liquor. The error of such acts are too apparent. He will be faced by less obvious temptations, like greed for power, self-glorification and complacency which are the little alcoholic foxes capable of stunting A.A. growth.

The road to happy, contented sobriety is often a rocky road filled with pitfalls and numerous obstructions over which we sometimes stumble and fall back to our old drinking habits. It seems that in spite of God's help, we insist upon plunging headlong into temptation.

Discussing this alcoholic characteristic with scores of A.A. members throughout the North American continent none of them believed that God was guilty of misleading them, or that He, in any way, obstructed their A.A. progress.

Their unanimous opinion was that we were the guilty offenders, and that the most sensible thing for us to do would be to ask God to deliver us from our self-imposed evil. Namely; from the insanity of alcoholism.

"FOR THINE IS THE KINGDOM AND THE POWER AND THE GLORY FOR EVER AND EVER"

It would be the height of presumption to assume that the foregoing concept of The Lord's Prayer is either correct, or complete. It is not, for only God Himself could give such an interpretation.

The thoughts presented simply represent one member's opinion of the manner in which this wonderful prayer works for him. They are intended to serve but one purpose, and that is to provide thought provoking suggestions to members who use the Lord's Prayer now and, hopefully, to those who may use it later.

Since God has chosen us to be His children it seems proper to reverently approach Him in prayer upon the level of a father and son basis. At least, those were our instructions when the prayer was given to us over nineteen centuries ago.

Viewing the matter in this respect, it seemingly rules out the supplicatory prayer in which we whine and beg our petitions for help, like a slave pleading to a cruel, relentless master. Nowhere in the prayer is such an inference indicated.

What is prayer? How do we pray? We reach the truest form of prayer when we become relaxed, and when we concentrate our minds upon the fact that we are talking to God. We should do more than just talk. Our prayer should be made in faith, and with the contemplation of an eventual answer — providing it will be helpful to us and will not harm another person.

It is not hard to believe that God expresses His good works through alcoholics who protect their sobriety by humble prayer, love, and by the service which they render to others. If this is the case, is it not most evident that He is really with us, performing a miracle in our lives? Many member believe that is exactly what happens.

Concentrating upon the marvelous construction of The Lord's Prayer, we are amazed to learn that it meets all of our spiritual needs at each member's intellectual level, and that it is offensive to nobody who believes in a Higher Power.

The last fifteen words of the prayer were not a part of the original prayer. They were probably added by monks many centuries ago, and have served as a practical affirmation ever since. They will probably remain in use because of their helpful supplementary value.

"For Thine Is The Kingdom," may have but little significance to us upon first consideration, but a study of this prayer requires more than a casual inspection. In one sense, "Thy Kingdom" could mean all of creation.

Our astronauts, in their flights into space, had great faith in the power of Almighty God which they carried to the moon, thus moving it beyond the earth. How much farther it will be carried is only a question of time, for the kingdom is large and there is plently of room in which to travel.

God's power is evidenced by many things both great and small ranging from the redwood seed which produces trees of enormous proportions, to the heartbeat of a newborn child. His power working through us transfigures every phase of our lives, *even changing alcoholic addiction into recovery from such addiction.*

If great honor, admiration and respect are won by performing apparently impossible acts, then certainly God qualifies for such honor, and for such glory for ever and ever. Amen.

NOTES

NOTES

NOTES

NOTES